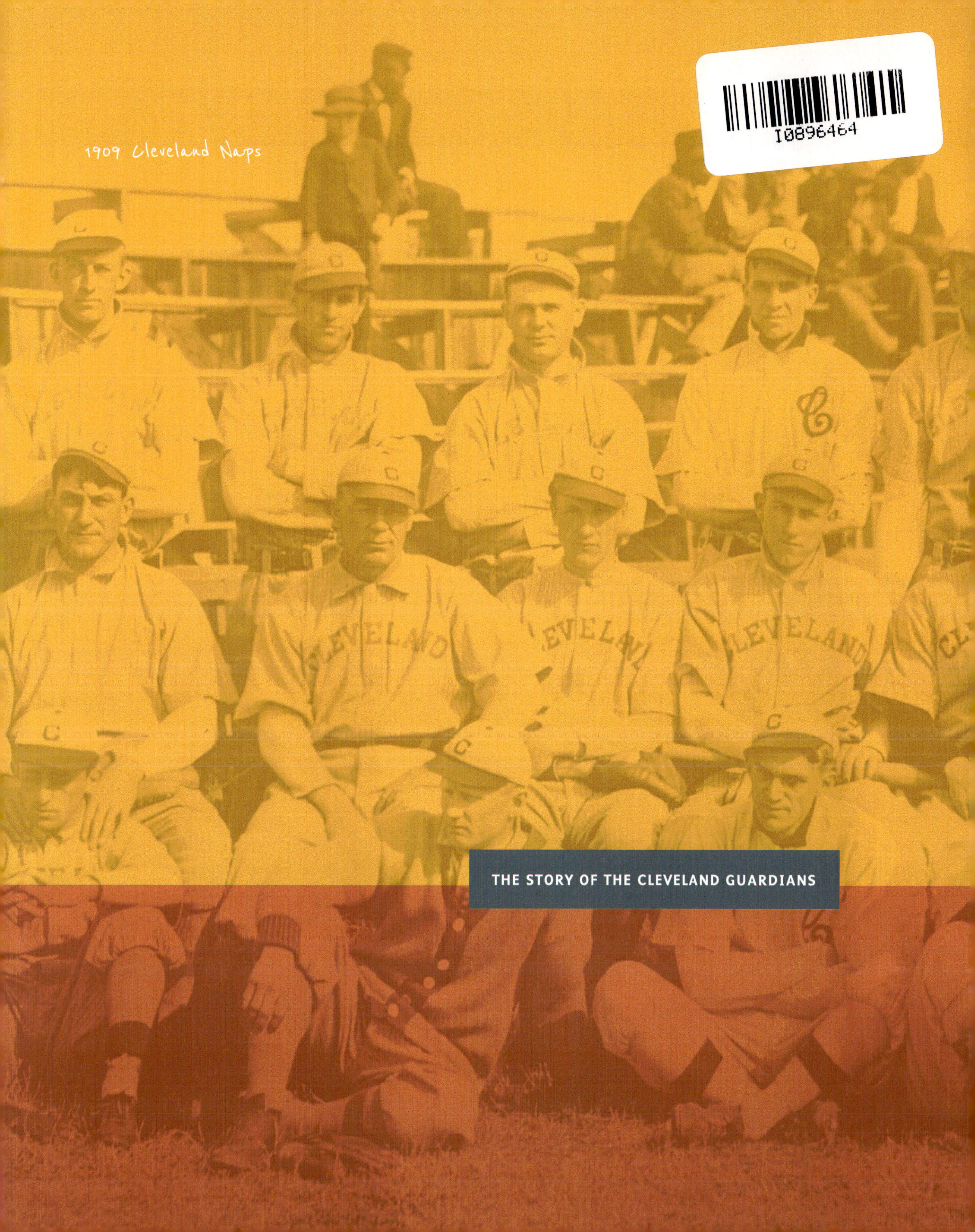

1909 Cleveland Naps

THE STORY OF THE CLEVELAND GUARDIANS

Pitcher Tanner Bibee

THE STORY OF THE

CLEVELAND GUARDIANS

JOE TISCHLER

Pitcher CC Sabathia

CREATIVE SPORTS

CREATIVE EDUCATION / CREATIVE PAPERBACKS

Published by Creative Education and Creative Paperbacks
P.O. Box 227, Mankato, Minnesota 56002
Creative Education and Creative Paperbacks are imprints of The Creative Company
www.thecreativecompany.us

Book Design by Graham Morgan
Art direction by Blue Design (www.bluedes.com)

Images by Alamy Stock Photo/McClatchy-Tribune, 26–27; Getty Images/Al Bello, 11, Al Fenn/Time Life Pictures, 7 (bottom, left), Bettmann, 20, Chris Bernacchi/Diamond Images, 30, Diamond Images, 6 (bottom, left), 29, G Newman Lowrance, 4–5, 32, George Silk/Time & Life Pictures, 16, Grace Hoppel, 2, Gregory Shamus, 7 (top, left), Hy Peskin/Time Life Pictures, 18, John Williamson, 7 (bottom, right), Jonathan Daniel, 3, 25, KIMBERLY BARTH, 22–23, Lauren Leigh Bacho, cover, Major League Baseball Photos, 12, National Baseball Hall of Fame Library, 15, Nick Cammett/Diamond Images, 31, Nick Laham, 6 (bottom, right), Photo File, cover, 6 (top, left), 19, Ron Vesely, 7 (top, right), TIMOTHY A. CLARY, 10, Tom Pidgeon, 9, TONY RANZE, 6 (top, right), 10; Wikimedia Commons/Bain News Service, 1

Library of Congress Cataloging-in-Publication Data
Names: Tischler, Joe author
Title: The story of the Cleveland Guardians / by Joe Tischler.
Description: Mankato, Minnesota : Creative Education and Creative Paperbacks, [2026] | Series: Creative sports. Major League baseball | Includes index. | Audience: Ages 8-12 | Audience: Grades 4-6 | Summary: "Discover the Cleveland Guardians' thrilling journey from early triumphs and integration milestones to recent rebranding, featuring legendary players, key events, and the Major League Baseball team's ongoing fan support. Written for middle-grade readers. Includes table of contents, sidebars, and index"– Provided by publisher.
Identifiers: LCCN 2025019592 (print) | LCCN 2025019593 (ebook) | ISBN 9798895810910 library binding | ISBN 9798896800446 paperback | ISBN 9798895812174 ebook
Subjects: LCSH: Cleveland Guardians (Baseball team)–History–Juvenile literature. | Cleveland Indians (Baseball team)–History–Juvenile literature. | World Series (Baseball) (1948)–Juvenile literature. | World Series (Baseball) (1954)–Juvenile literature. | American League of Professional Baseball Clubs–History–Juvenile literature. | Major League Baseball (Organization)–History–Juvenile literature.
Classification: LCC GV875.C7 T574 2026 (print) | LCC GV875.C7 (ebook) | DDC 796.357/640977132–dc23/eng/20250620
LC record available at https://lccn.loc.gov/2025019592
LC ebook record available at https://lccn.loc.gov/2025019593

Printed in the United States

Center fielder Grady Sizemore

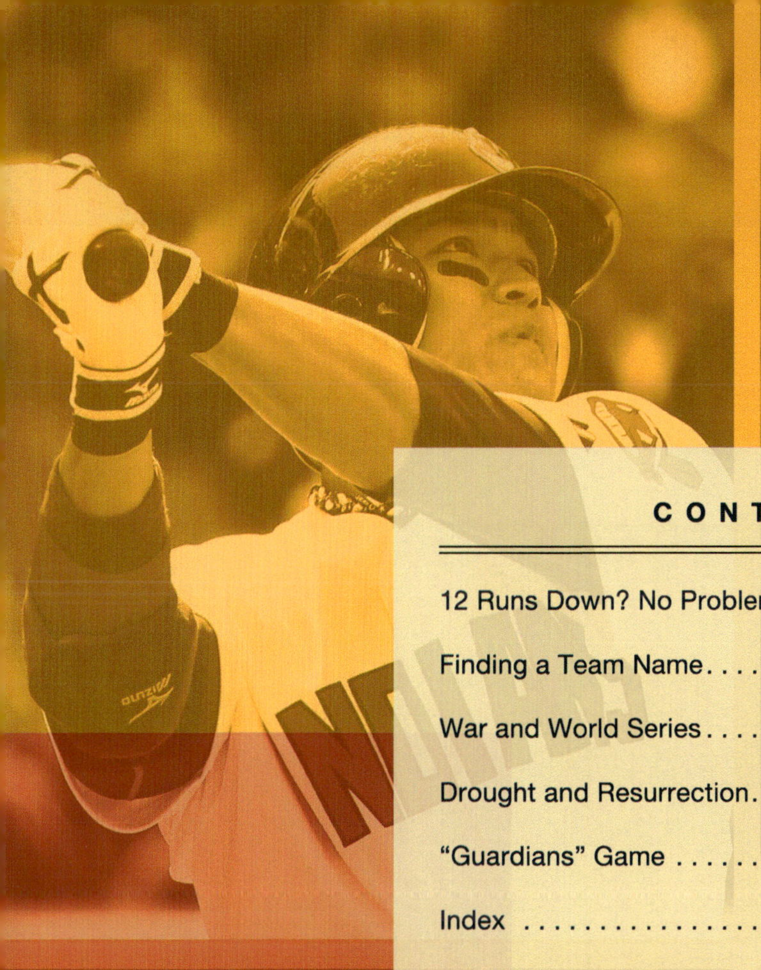

CONTENTS

12 Runs Down? No Problem 8

Finding a Team Name 13

War and World Series 17

Drought and Resurrection 21

“Guardians” Game 24

Index 32

EXTRA INNINGS

A “Natural” Home Run Hitter 10

A Tight Finish 15

Ageless Wonder 16

War to World Series Hero 20

Cy Young Rotation 27

Movie Mayhem 29

12 RUNS DOWN? NO PROBLEM

It did not seem like it was the Cleveland Indians night. On August 5, 2001, Cleveland hosted the Seattle Mariners in the third game of a four-game series. Seattle won the first two games of the series. It did a lot of winning in 2001. Going into the game, the Mariners were a startling 50 games over .500 (80–30). They went on to win 116 games that year. It tied a major league record for wins in a season.

As expected, Seattle jumped ahead of Cleveland early. It scored four runs in the second inning. Then the Mariners scored eight more times in the third. They led 12–0 after three innings. Cleveland got on the board in the bottom of the fourth. Future Hall of Famer Jim Thome hit a two-run home run. The lead was cut to 10 at 12–2. Seattle got those runs back in the fifth to regain their 12-run advantage at 14–2.

The game was well in hand for Seattle. According to Baseball-Reference, Cleveland had less than a one percent chance of winning. The largest comeback in Major League Baseball (MLB) history was 12 runs. It had only happened twice. But the last time it occurred was 1925, 76 years prior. Both teams soon began replacing their starters with reserve players.

First baseman/designated hitter Jim Thome

EXTRA INNINGS

JIM THOME
FIRST BASEMAN/DESIGNATED HITTER
GUARDIANS SEASONS: 1991–2002, 2011
HEIGHT: 6-FOOT-4
WEIGHT: 250 POUNDS
KEY STATS: 2018 HALL OF FAME INDUCTEE, 612 CAREER HOME RUNS, 5X ALL-STAR, SILVER SLUGGER AWARD

A "NATURAL" HOME RUN HITTER

Only nine players in MLB history have hit over 600 career home runs. Jim Thome is one of them. His 612 career home runs rank eighth all time. He had a unique batting stance that he mimicked from the movie *The Natural*. The left-handed batter held his bat out with his right hand, pointing it to right field until just before the pitch was thrown. Thome was not much of a home run hitter at first. He only hit 10 home runs during his first three seasons. His power came in 1994. He belted 20 that year. His yearly totals kept climbing. He launched a career-high 52 in 2002. Thome had a great attitude on and off the field. He won multiple awards for his community service.

Shortstop Omar Vizquel (L) and Left fielder Albert Belle (R)

The score remained 14–2 going into the bottom of the seventh. One of Cleveland's reserves got the team's rally started. Russell Branyan led off the inning with a home run. Another reserve, Jolbert Cabrera, later drove in a pair with a single. The score was 14–5 after the seventh inning.

Seattle did not score in the top of the eighth. Jim Thome hit his second home run of the game to lead off the bottom half. Marty Cordova followed with a two-run home run. Omar Vizquel later added an RBI double. Seattle led 14–9 going to the ninth inning.

Rich Rodriguez came on to pitch the ninth for Cleveland. He retired all three Seattle batters he faced. Cleveland was down to its final turn at-bat. Ed Taubensee started the ninth with a single. The next two batters were retired. The Indians were down to their final out. They still needed five runs. Cordova kept the game going with a double. Wil Cordero walked to load the bases. Einar Díaz singled to bring in two runs. The score was now 14–11. Kenny Lofton singled. The bases were loaded again. Vizquel was at bat. On a 3–2 count, Vizquel hit a shot down the right field line. All three runners came across to score. Vizquel was safe at third. Remarkably, the game was tied!

The game went to extra innings. It remained 14–14 in the bottom of the 11th inning. With two runners on and one out, Cabrera hit a broken-bat single to left field, and Lofton scored from second for the winning run. Cleveland won 15–14. "Cabrera got the base hit and I scored and the next thing you know, we're going crazy," said Lofton. "This is going to be the comeback of the century. It was pretty much that. Once I scored, I was like, 'Wow.'"

FINDING A TEAM NAME

In 1901, eight teams formed the new American League (AL). One franchise was located in Cleveland, Ohio. Its players wore blue uniforms. Owners named the team Bluebirds or "Blues." Players hated the name. It was changed to Broncos the following year. That did not stick either. The team struggled on the field while trying to find a team name. It finished seventh and fifth place those two seasons.

Napoleon Lajoie joined the franchise in 1902. He was one of baseball's first superstars. In 1901, while playing for the Philadelphia Athletics, he won the Triple Crown. That is where a batter leads the league in three categories: batting average, home runs, and runs batted in (RBI). He hit a remarkable .426 in 1901. That remains an AL record. Lajoie batted .379 in his first season in Cleveland. Sportswriters began calling the team the Napoleons, or "Naps" for short. "Nap" was Lajoie's nickname. That team name became official before the 1903 season. Lajoie led the AL in batting in 1903 and 1904. In 1905, he took on the role of player/manager.

Cleveland had winning records under Lajoie. But the team failed to win the pennant. He stepped down as manager during the 1909 season.

Center fielder Tris Speaker

He stayed on as a player. Lajoie's last season in Cleveland was 1914. That meant the franchise needed a new name. Local sportswriters suggested Indians. Cleveland had a National League (NL) team in the late 1800s. It briefly had an American Indian on the team named Louis Sockalexis. He was the first American Indian in the league. So people sometimes referred to the team as the "Indians." The team name was established.

Before the 1916 season, the Indians traded for center fielder Tris Speaker. He played close to second base. The trade seemed worth it. He led MLB in batting his first season in Cleveland with a .386 average. Speaker became a player/manager during the 1919 season. The team finished in second place.

Expectations were high going into 1920. Tragedy struck in August. Talented shortstop Ray Chapman was killed after taking a pitch to the head. Batting helmets were not worn during this time. Grieving their teammate's death, the Indians faltered in the standings. They rallied down the stretch, winning 24 of their last 32 games. Cleveland won its first AL pennant. The team faced the Brooklyn Robins (later known as Dodgers) in the World Series. The Indians lost two of the first three games of the best-of-nine series. The next four games were played in Cleveland. The Robins scored only two runs over those games. Cleveland won all four games. The Indians captured their first world championship.

The rest of the 1920s featured fine efforts from such players as shortstop Joe Sewell. The 1921 and 1926 teams finished second in the AL. First baseman George Burns was named AL Most Valuable Player (MVP) in 1926.

EXTRA INNINGS

A TIGHT FINISH

Nap Lajoie and Ty Cobb of the Detroit Tigers were neck and neck for the 1910 AL batting crown. The Chalmers Motor Company promised a car to the winner. It came down to the final game of the season. Cobb sat out. Cleveland played a doubleheader against the St. Louis Browns. By most players, Cobb was hated. Lajoie was admired. Lajoie bunted his way on base seven times. The Sporting News stated that Cobb's average was .384944. Lajoie's was .384084. Chalmers gave both players a car anyway. It was eventually discovered that the totals had been calculated wrong. Lajoie was the actual champion.

NAPOLEON "NAP" LAJOIE
SECOND BASEMAN
GUARDIANS SEASONS: 1902–14
HEIGHT: 6-FOOT-1
WEIGHT: 195 POUNDS
KEY STATS: 1937 HALL OF FAME INDUCTEE, 5X BATTING TITLE, .338 CAREER BATTING AVERAGE, 3X RBI LEADER

EXTRA INNINGS

SATCHEL PAIGE
PITCHER
GUARDIANS SEASONS: 1948–49
HEIGHT: 6-FOOT-3
WEIGHT: 180 POUNDS
KEY STATS: 1971 HALL OF FAME INDUCTEE, 2X MLB ALL-STAR, 1948 WORLD SERIES CHAMPION, OLDEST PLAYER IN MLB HISTORY

AGELESS WONDER

As a child, Leroy Paige worked as a railroad baggage handler. He soon earned his nickname, "Satchel." He was sent to reform school when he was 13. While there, he learned how to pitch. Paige became an excellent pitcher in the Negro Leagues. But for a long time, the AL and NL were rigidly segregated. He could not pitch in those leagues. Paige finally got his chance in 1948 at the age of 41. The Indians signed him. He pitched in 21 games that year, compiling a 6–1 record. He became the first Black pitcher to play in the World Series. He made history again in 1965. Kansas City Athletics owner Charlie Finley signed Paige for one game. He was 59 years old. He was the oldest player in MLB history. Paige pitched three innings and allowed only one hit.

WAR AND WORLD SERIES

The early 1930s brought a new home for the Indians. On July 31, 1932, the 78,000-seat Cleveland Municipal Stadium opened. "When I went to the mound and looked around at the crowd, it was the most awesome thing I'd ever seen," recalled pitcher Mel Harder. "It was hard to believe so many people could be in one place."

In 1936, fans had a young pitcher to cheer for. Cleveland signed 17-year-old Bob Feller. "Rapid Robert" lived up to his nickname. He had a sizzling fastball. It became the stuff of legend. Feller led the AL in strikeouts seven times. In 1940, Feller was hitting his peak. He threw a no-hitter on Opening Day. He went on to win the pitching Triple Crown. He led the AL with 27 wins, a 2.61 earned-run average (ERA), and totaled 261 strikeouts. Cleveland battled with Detroit all year for the AL pennant. But the Tigers edged out Cleveland by one game.

Feller went on military duty during World War II. He missed three full seasons. He returned in 1946 and was still in top form. He won 26 games and struck out a franchise-record 348 batters.

New Cleveland owner Bill Veeck was at the forefront of integrating the major leagues. In 1947, Jackie Robinson of the NL's Brooklyn Dodgers became the first Black player in MLB. A year later, Cleveland's Larry Doby broke the AL color barrier. Before Doby's first game, shortstop/manager Lou Boudreau introduced him to his new teammates. "All the guys put their hand out, all but three," Doby said. "As soon as he could, Bill Veeck got rid of those three."

Center fielder Larry Doby

Veeck later signed pitcher Satchel Paige. He had been a sensation for many years in the Negro Leagues.

Bob Lemon joined Feller in the Cleveland pitching rotation in 1946. Two years later, Lemon was key in helping a pennant push. He led the majors with 10 shutouts. Cleveland tied Boston for the AL lead at the end of the season. A one-game tiebreaker was needed. The Indians won, 8–3. They returned to the World Series for the first time in 28 years.

Cleveland faced the Boston Braves. The Indians lost the first game. Stellar pitching allowed them to win the next three games. They allowed only two runs over those games. Boston won the next game to stay alive in the best-of-seven series. Cleveland responded in Game 6. Gene Bearden recorded the save as the Indians won 4–3. They claimed their second world championship.

Cleveland returned to the World Series in 1954. They won a then-AL-record 111 games. The Indians faced the New York Giants. Game 1 was highlighted by one of the greatest catches in MLB history by Giants' center fielder Willie Mays. The catch saved at least two runs. Cleveland lost in extra innings. They lost the next three games, too. New York swept the series.

Pitcher Bob Feller

EXTRA INNINGS

GENE BEARDEN
PITCHER
GUARDIANS SEASONS: 1947–50
HEIGHT: 6-FOOT-3
WEIGHT: 204 POUNDS
KEY STATS: 1948 ERA TITLE, 1948 WORLD SERIES CHAMPION, 3.96 CAREER ERA, 259 CAREER STRIKEOUTS

WAR TO WORLD SERIES HERO

Gene Bearden served in the U.S. Navy during World War II. There are many stories about his involvement, but not all of them are true. Some reports say he fractured his skull and crushed his kneecap when the ship he was on sank. He reportedly spent nearly two years in a hospital. That story, however, was not verified. What is true is that he was a vital member of Cleveland's 1948 World Series win. A rookie in 1948, Bearden won 20 games. His 2.43 ERA led the AL. He was runner-up in Rookie of the Year voting. In the World Series, Bearden pitched a complete-game shutout in Game 3. He then came in relief during the series-clinching Game 6 and recorded the save.

DROUGHT AND RESURRECTION

Cleveland came close to a return trip to the World Series in the later part of the 1950s. It finished in second place three times. The last time was in 1959. Right fielder Rocky Colavito slugged over 40 home runs in 1958 and 1959. He was a fan favorite. He stayed at the ballpark for long autograph sessions after each game. But Cleveland traded him to Detroit prior to the 1960 season. The Indians fell to fourth place.

This was the beginning of a long stretch of mediocre baseball in Cleveland. The club brought Colavito back in 1965. But his hitting steadily declined. One player the Indians traded for Colavito was pitcher Tommy John. John went on to win 286 games for other teams. This imbalance was typical of many Cleveland trades during this era. The team seemed to give away its best players, receiving little in return.

The league split into two divisions in 1969. Cleveland was in the AL East Division. Throughout the next 25 years, the Indians had just four winning seasons. In 1991, they lost a franchise-record 105 games.

Three years after that, the Indians moved out of their longtime home, Cleveland Municipal Stadium. They moved into Jacobs Field (now called Progressive Field). They also moved to the newly formed AL Central Division. The change of scenery inspired the players. The team started winning. In early August, the Indians trailed the White Sox by just one game for the division lead. But a players' strike ended the season.

Outfielder David Justice

The strike carried over into 1995. The season started late. Teams played 144 games instead of the usual 162. Still, Cleveland won 100 games. It easily won the division. This marked the franchise's first playoff appearance in 41 years. Six starting players had batting averages above .300. Big catcher Sandy Alomar Jr. and sure-gloved shortstop Omar Vizquel led Cleveland's defense. The Indians swept the Boston Red Sox in the AL Division Series (ALDS). Then they beat the Seattle Mariners in the AL Championship Series (ALCS). The Indians were finally back in the World Series. They faced the Atlanta Braves. Atlanta's superior pitching prevailed. The Braves held the hot-hitting Indians to a .179 team batting average. Atlanta won in six games.

Cleveland stormed to an MLB-best 99 wins the following season. But the wild-card Baltimore Orioles won in the ALDS. The Indians topped the AL Central again in 1997. They beat the New York Yankees and Baltimore in the playoffs. The team made its second World Series appearance in three years. It faced the Florida Marlins. The series came down to Game 7. It stretched into extra innings. Florida scored the winning run in the bottom of the 11th inning. Cleveland's hopes were crushed again.

"GUARDIANS" GAME

Power-hitting outfielder Manny Ramírez carried much of the offense in 1999. He set a team record with a whopping 165 RBI. Cleveland became just the third team to win five straight division titles. But the Red Sox topped them in the ALDS.

Outfielder Manny Ramírez

RAMIREZ
24

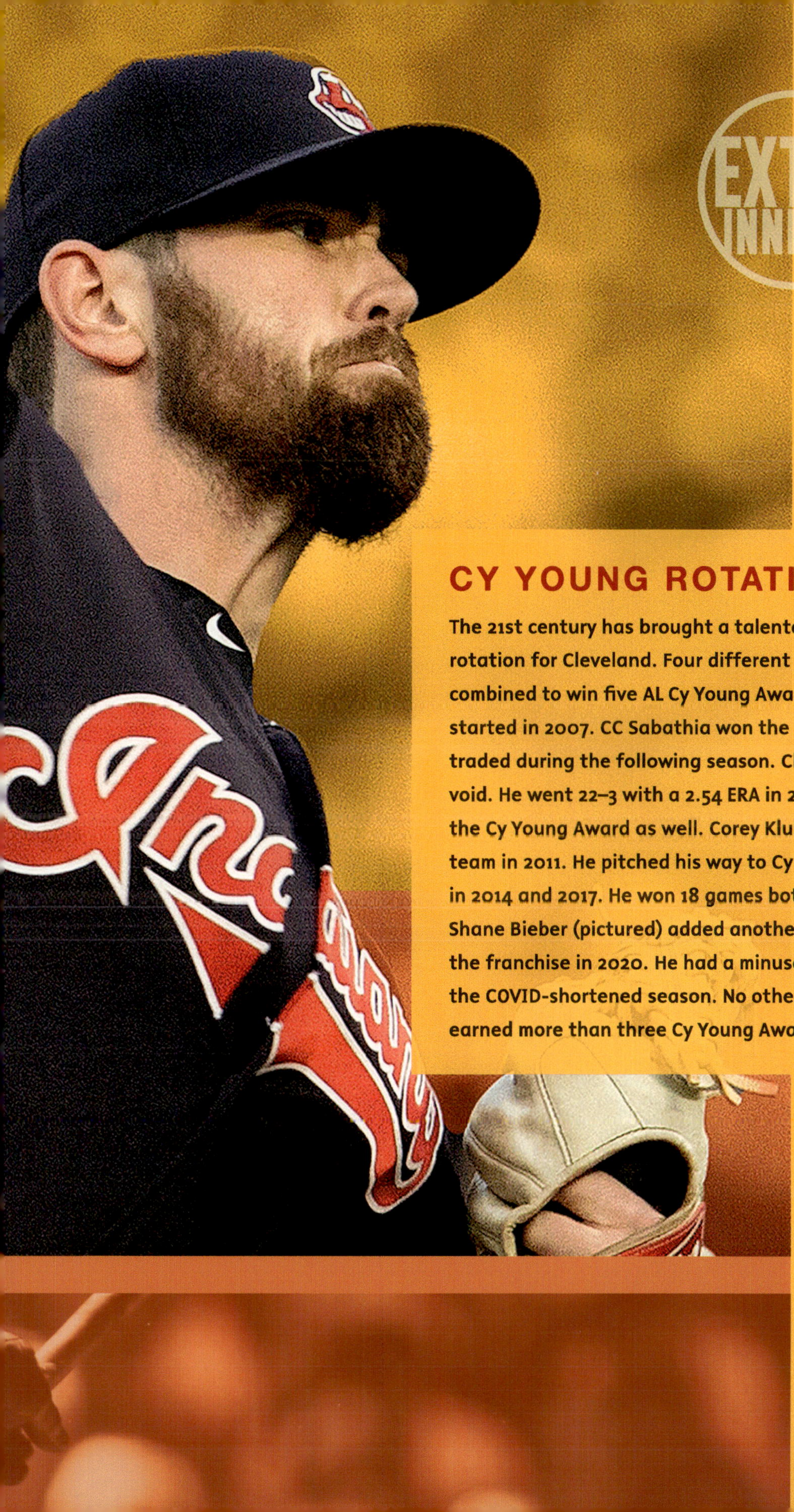

EXTRA INNINGS

CY YOUNG ROTATION

The 21st century has brought a talented pitching rotation for Cleveland. Four different pitchers have combined to win five AL Cy Young Awards. The trend started in 2007. CC Sabathia won the award. He was traded during the following season. Cliff Lee filled the void. He went 22–3 with a 2.54 ERA in 2008. He won the Cy Young Award as well. Corey Kluber joined the team in 2011. He pitched his way to Cy Young Awards in 2014 and 2017. He won 18 games both seasons. Shane Bieber (pictured) added another Cy Young to the franchise in 2020. He had a minuscule 1.63 ERA in the COVID-shortened season. No other AL team has earned more than three Cy Young Awards since 2000.

Ramírez left before the 2001 season. First baseman Jim Thome picked up the slack. The lefty clubbed 49 home runs. Cleveland earned another trip to the postseason. It took the 116-win Seattle Mariners to a deciding fifth game in the ALDS. But the Mariners prevailed. Cleveland fell below .500 the following season for the first time in nine seasons. It had losing records in three of the next four years.

In 2007, Cleveland returned to the top of the division. It mowed down the Yankees in the ALDS. Cleveland took a 3–1 series lead over Boston in the ALCS. But the Red Sox dominated the final three games to oust Cleveland.

Five straight non-winning seasons followed. One bright spot was pitcher Cliff Lee. He went 22–3 in 2008. He captured the AL Cy Young Award. Terry Francona took over as manager in 2013. He had managed two world championship teams with Boston. He led Cleveland to the playoffs in his first season with the team. But it lost to Tampa Bay in the AL Wild Card Game.

Cleveland returned to the postseason in 2016. It easily advanced through the AL playoffs. It swept Boston in the ALDS. Then it topped the Toronto Blue Jays in five games in the ALCS. The Indians met the Chicago Cubs in the World Series. Both teams had long world championship droughts. The Indians hadn't won since 1948. The Cubs hadn't won since 1908. Cleveland won three of the first four games. The Cubs won the next two to force a Game 7. Rajai Davis's eighth-inning three-run home run tied the game and helped send it into extra innings. The Cubs scored twice in the 10th inning. Cleveland only countered with one. Chicago won 8–7. Cleveland's championship drought continued.

The Indians returned to the playoffs in the COVID-shortened 2020 season. The season was cut from 162 games to 60. Cleveland went 35–25. It hosted the Yankees in the AL Wild Card Series. But New York swept the best-of-three series.

Prior to the 2022 season, the franchise underwent a facelift. After being known as the Indians for over 100 years, the team changed its name to

MOVIE MAYHEM

The 1989 movie *Major League* offered a fictional account of the Cleveland Indians. In the film, a money-hungry widow has inherited the team. She wants to move the team to Florida. She tries to drive fan support down by throwing together a roster full of losers and has-beens. Predictably, yet comically, the misfits come together to find success. They save both the season and the franchise for Cleveland. The movie was a surprise hit. *New York Times* reviewer Caryn James wrote, "*Major League* trots out the standard formula but has the wit to make fun of it now and then." The success of the movie brought two sequels.

Third baseman José Ramírez

Guardians. The name references the "Guardians of Traffic." These are eight sculptures on the city's Hope Memorial Bridge near Progressive Field.

The team surged to a division title under its new name in 2022. Third baseman José Ramírez led a balanced Cleveland attack. He drove in 126 runs. Cleveland swept the Tampa Bay Rays in the AL Wild Card Series. But the Guardians fell again to the Yankees in the ALDS.

Francona resigned as manager following the next season. Stephen Vogt was named manager. He helped return the Guardians to the top of the AL Central in 2024. Ramírez and first baseman Josh Naylor each drove in over 100 runs. Closer Emmanuel Clase topped the AL with 47 saves. The Guardians beat Detroit in the ALDS. But, again, the Yankees knocked them out of the playoffs in the ALCS.

Cleveland's rich baseball history goes back more than 140 years. Though the Guardians have not hoisted a World Series trophy since 1948, fans refuse to give up hope. When Cleveland claims its next championship, the victory will be all the sweeter.

First baseman Kyle Manzardo

INDEX

AL Championship Series (ALCS), 24, 28, 31
AL Division Series (ALDS), 24, 28, 31
AL Wild Card Series, 28, 31
Alomar, Sandy, Jr., 24
Bearden, Gene, 18, 20
Bieber, Shane, 27
Boudreau, Lou, 17
Branyan, Russell, 11
Burns, George, 14
Cabrera, Jolbert, 11, 13
Chapman, Ray, 14
Clase, Emmanuel, 31
Cleveland Municipal Stadium, 17, 21
Colavito, Rocky, 21
Cordero, Wil, 11
Cordova, Marty, 11
COVID-19, 27, 28
Cy Young Award, 27, 28
Davis, Rajai, 28
Diaz, Einar, 11
Doby, Larry, 17, 18
Feller, Bob, 17, 18, 19
Francona, Terry, 28, 31
Harder, Mel, 17
John, Tommy, 21
Kluber, Corey, 27
Lajoie, Napoleon, 13, 14, 15
Lee, Cliff, 27, 28
Lemon, Bob, 18
Lofton, Kenny, 11, 13
Major League, 29
Most Valuable Player (MVP), 14
Naylor, Josh, 31
no-hitter, 17
Paige, Satchel, 16, 18
Progressive Field (Jacobs Field), 21, 31
Ramirez, Jose, 31
Ramirez, Manny, 24, 25
Rodriguez, Rich, 11
Rookie of the Year, 20
Sabathia, CC, 3, 27
Sewell, Joe, 14
Sockalexis, Louis, 14
Speaker, Tris, 13, 14
Taubensee, Ed, 11
Thome, Jim, 8, 9, 10, 11, 28
Triple Crown, 13, 17
Veeck, Bill, 17, 18
Vizquel, Omar, 11, 24
Vogt, Stephen, 31
World Series, 14, 16, 17, 18, 20, 21, 24, 28, 31
World Series champions, 16, 20